Jeffrey Smith

THE BOOK OF FANTASTIC PLANES

Illustrated by
ROY COOMBS

Written by
NICHOLAS de VERE

Copyright © 1974 The Archon Press Limited, London
U.S. edition published 1974 by Golden Press, New York Western Publishing Company, Inc. Printed in U.S.A.
All rights reserved. Golden, A Golden Book ®, and Golden Press ® are trademarks of Western Publishing Company, Inc.
Library of Congress Catalog Card Number: 73-92287
ISBN: 0 307 12676 5

GOLDEN PRESS · NEW YORK
Western Publishing Company, Inc.
Racine, Wisconsin

INTRODUCTION

For thousands of years, man dreamed of being able to fly. He envied birds and their freedom of the skies, and longed to fly too. It is not surprising then, that from early times it was thought that the secret of flight lay in being able to construct bird-like wings, attaching them to the arms of a man who would fly by merely flapping them in the wind. An early Greek legend tells how Icarus and Daedalus attempted to escape from the Isle of Crete by flying with wings made of bird feathers stuck to their arms by wax. Men were reluctant to abandon their idea of wings and hundreds of years passed before a more practical approach to flight was conceived. Around A.D. 1500, Leonardo da Vinci, the great Italian painter and sculptor, drew plans for a flying machine. Although this was never built, experts who have studied da Vinci's drawings say that if there had been a suitable source of power, his machine could have flown.

In many lands, brave men risked and sometimes lost their lives in their attempts to fly. However, after years of failure, man actually rose into the air and stayed there for a reasonable period of time in 1783 when a balloon filled with hot air was used. From this first achievement, over 100 years passed before the first powered airplane flight was made in 1903 near Kill Devil Hill, Kitty Hawk, North Carolina by Orville and Wilbur Wright. This great feat was followed by a surge of enthusiasm resulting in the production of some incredible aircraft, particularly in France. Another turning point in the development of the airplane was the First World War. By 1918, planes were efficient and effective fighters as well as flying machines. The imagination of the entire world was captured in 1919 when Alcock and Brown flew the Atlantic; and the years between World Wars I and II saw very rapid development of aircraft as shown by the creation of such planes as the huge Dornier, the GB Super Sportster, and the record-breaking Supermarine S6B.

From these first years of airplane flight when speeds were no greater than 35 m.p.h. and distances covered were measured in feet, man has created planes that fly higher, faster and longer than the Wright brothers could ever have dreamed possible. It is hard to realize that the invention of the airplane spans no more than a lifetime and that from the first frail airplane the huge Skycrane, the MiG 23, and the supersonic Concorde have developed. Within the pages of this book are numerous examples of the many aircraft that helped blaze the trail that has led man to his boldest adventure—the conquest of space.

Some words that may be unfamiliar are explained in the glossary at the back of this book.

TROUVÉ ORNITHOPTER 1870

Country: France. **Size:** a model only.
This was a successful attempt to imitate the flapping wings of birds in flight.

The Frenchman, Gustave Trouvé, thought that the secret of flight lay in being able to build a machine whose wings flapped. He reasoned that if birds could achieve flight like this, then man, with the aid of a machine, could do it too. He built a model machine with flapping wings, which was the first of its kind to fly.

This type of machine became known as an ornithopter. Its wing mechanism was worked by the firing of 12 blank revolver cartridges, each powering a single flap of the wings. Remarkably, it was able to fly in this way and after a mid-air launch, actually propelled itself for 200 feet.

DU TEMPLE 1874

Country: France. **Size:** wing span 55 ft. 7 in., 32 ft. 8 in. long, propeller diameter 13 ft.
Engine: Steam.
It made the first powered flight.

The first successful powered aircraft in history was designed by Felix du Temple. Built as a model, the plane was powered first by clockwork, then by steam. It was able to take off under its own power, sustain itself in flight and above all, land in safety. From this model another historically important machine evolved—the first full-sized powered airplane. Piloted by a young sailor at Brest, the plane roller-coasted down a slope and made a short hop, landing with a bump.

This was too short to be considered a flight, but nevertheless, it was the first powered, piloted airplane to leave the ground.

WRIGHT FLYER I
1903

Country: U.S.A. **Size:** wing span 40 ft. 4 in., 21 ft. 1 in. long, 8 ft. high and 605 lbs. (empty).
Engine: one 12 h.p. **Speed:** 30–35 m.p.h.
It was the first plane to achieve true flight.

After many unsuccessful attempts with man-carrying kites, Wilbur and Orville Wright built this airplane, with an engine also of their own design. Watched by an audience of five coastguards and a photographer, Orville lay on the bottom wing of the controls while Wilbur ran along the ground holding one wing-tip. The flyer flew for just 12 seconds and 120 feet, but sustained flight had been achieved.

PHILLIPS I 1904

Country: Great Britain.
Size: wing span 17 ft. 9 in.,
13 ft. 4 in. long, 10 ft. high
and 600 lbs.
Engine: one 22 h.p.
**It made the first 'hop'
flight in Britain.**

Horatio Phillips was one of
the first people to study the
shape of a wing, and to
test out his theories he built
the world's first wind tunnel.
His aircraft, which you can
see here, resembled a motor-
ized venetian blind. But in
this incredible machine
Phillips claims to have made
a 'hop' flight of about 500
feet, becoming the first man
in Britain to fly.

VUIA NUMBER I (Monoplane) 1906

Country: Rumania.
Size: wing span 28 ft. 7 in.,
9 ft. 10 in. long and 531 lbs.
Engine: one 25 h.p. Serpollet
carbonic acid gas.
It had wings like a bat.

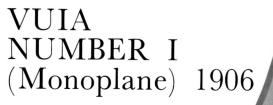

From another part of the world, Transylvania (now Rumania), came
another pioneer, Trajan Vuia, who took up residence in Paris. There he
built this aircraft in 1906, which only succeeded in making 'hop' flights.
Despite this failure, Vuia influenced later pioneers, notably Blériot, with
the basic design of his aircraft. The wings resembled bats' wings and were
controlled by wires, which warped the edges when pulled.

ELLEHAMMER II 1906

Country: Denmark. **Size:** wing span 30 ft. 11¾ in., 20 ft. 4⅛ in. long, 10 ft. 8¾ in. high and 397 lbs.
Engine: one 20 h.p. Ellehammer 3-cylinder air-cooled radial. **Speed:** 35 m.p.h.
It made the first 'claimed' flight in Europe.

On the island of Lindholm, on a circular track, 33 feet in diameter, with his plane tethered to the center on a wire, Jacob Christian Ellehammer made a flight of 138 feet. His friends claimed this as the first manned flight in Europe. But Ellehammer could hardly be said to have piloted the plane, being more a passenger. Ellehammer built more aircraft but none flew and his backers lost confidence in him and he was forced to give up his attempts to build machines that would fly.

SANTOS-DUMONT 14BIS 1906

Country: Brazil/France. **Size:** wing span 36 ft. 9 in., 31 ft. 10 in. long, and 661 lbs. **Engine:** one 50 h.p. Antoinette 8-cylinder water-cooled. **Speed:** approx. 25 m.p.h.
It made the first true flight in Europe.

Inspired by the Wrights, Alberto Santos-Dumont, a Brazilian builder of airships, built this bi-plane. It was the first of many planes that he built (see following page) and he made two tests before attempting to pilot it. In the first, the aircraft was strung up on an overhead wire and pulled by a donkey! In the second, the aircraft was suspended beneath one of Santos-Dumont's airships. After the tests he took his machine to Bagatelle near Paris and on October 23, 1906 made one 'hop-flight' of 197 feet. Two weeks later, he flew again and covered 722 feet in a flight of 21⅓ seconds. This achievement won him a silver cup, a prize of 1,500 francs and fame as the first European to fly.

SANTOS-DUMONT DEMOISELLE 1907

Country: Brazil/France. **Size:** wing span 16 ft. 5 in. and 242 lbs.
Engine: 2-cylinder Dutheil-Chalmers 20 h.p. **Speed:** 25 m.p.h.
It was the first successful monoplane.

Not satisfied with his bi-plane achievements, Santos-Dumont set about the design of a single-winged machine. In 1907, he built the first of his light planes known as the 'Dragonfly'. It was made of canvas and struts of bamboo. Santos-Dumont hoped his design would become the world's first do-it-yourself aircraft kit. The plane made three 'hops', the longest being 654 feet, but then crashed. Two years later Santos-Dumont came out with an improved design, which managed flight of up to 10 minutes in tests. The plane was offered for sale for $750.00, and undoubtedly paved the way for future enthusiasts wishing to fly a light sporty machine.

BLÉRIOT XI 1909

Country: France. **Size:** wing span 25 ft. 7 in., 26 ft.
3 in. long and 463 lbs.
Engine: 3-cylinder 23 h.p. Anzani. **Speed:** 45 m.p.h.
**It made the first flight
across the English
Channel.**

It was in this plane that Louis Blériot made
the historic first airplane crossing of
the English Channel on July 25, 1909. He
flew the 26 miles from Les Baraques,
France, to a meadow near Dover Castle,
England, in $36\frac{1}{2}$ minutes. His
achievement was all the more remarkable
considering he had no compass. Flying only
feet above the water, he is reputed to have lost
his way and to complicate matters, his engine
began to over-heat dangerously. Disaster was
averted by a timely rainstorm which cooled the
engine and allowed him to reach England. Sceptics
discount this story, although none deny him the
honor of being the first to make this historic flight.

FABRE SEAPLANE HYDRAVION 1910

Country: France. **Size:** wing span 45 ft. 11 in., 27 ft. 11 in. long and 1,047 lbs.
Engine: one 50 h.p. Gnome 7-cylinder rotary. **Speed:** 55 m.p.h.
It was the first seaplane to fly.

In the early days of aviation there were few airports and the ones that existed always seemed far from city centers. It was a Frenchman, Henri Fabre, from a shipbuilding family, who decided the answer was to use the world's seas and waterways. He set about building a seaplane. His shipping background clearly influenced the plane he built, especially in the use he made of canvas as a covering for the wings. On March 28, 1910, Fabre perched atop this structure like a cowboy on a seahorse, and started the engine. The plane skimmed along the waters of Martigues near Marseilles and eventually lifted itself off the surface. It was an historic moment.

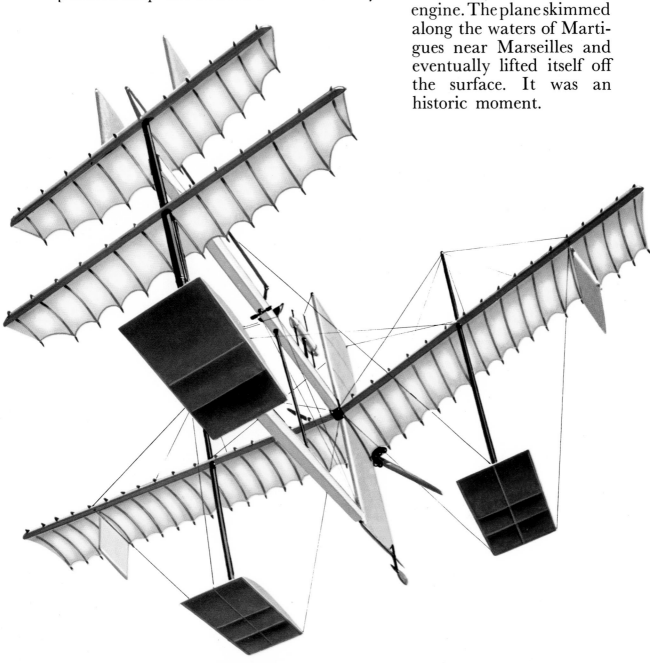

SIKORSKY 'LE GRAND' 1913

Country: Russia. **Size:** 65 ft. 8 in. long and 5,950 lbs.
Engine: four 100 h.p. 4-cylinder Argus water-cooled. **Speed:** 55 m.p.h.
It was the first passenger-carrying aircraft.

There were few Russian pioneers of flight but a notable one was Igor Sikorsky. He had experimented with helicopters at the beginning of the century but he temporarily put aside this idea to build 'Le Grand'. It was by far the largest heavier-than-air craft built at that time, the first 4-engined aircraft to fly, and the first to have a passenger cabin. Experts told Sikorsky that his machine would be too dangerous, as no plane could be flown from an enclosed cabin. The first flight lasted only ten minutes on May 13, 1913. Sikorsky piloted the plane and in view of the experts' warning, he had a man to stand outside, in an area in front of the cockpit, and signal altitude changes during the flight. Inside the cabin was a second pilot, whose job was to move forward or aft if the aircraft proved nose or tail heavy. On August 2, a modified version flew for nearly two hours. The outrider was abandoned, and in addition to Sikorsky there were eight passengers, who enjoyed the comfort of four armchairs, a sofa and a table. Another notable first was the use of a dual control system. Shortly after these historic flights, Sikorsky fled Russia and settled in America, where he went back to building the helicopters with which his name has now become synonymous.

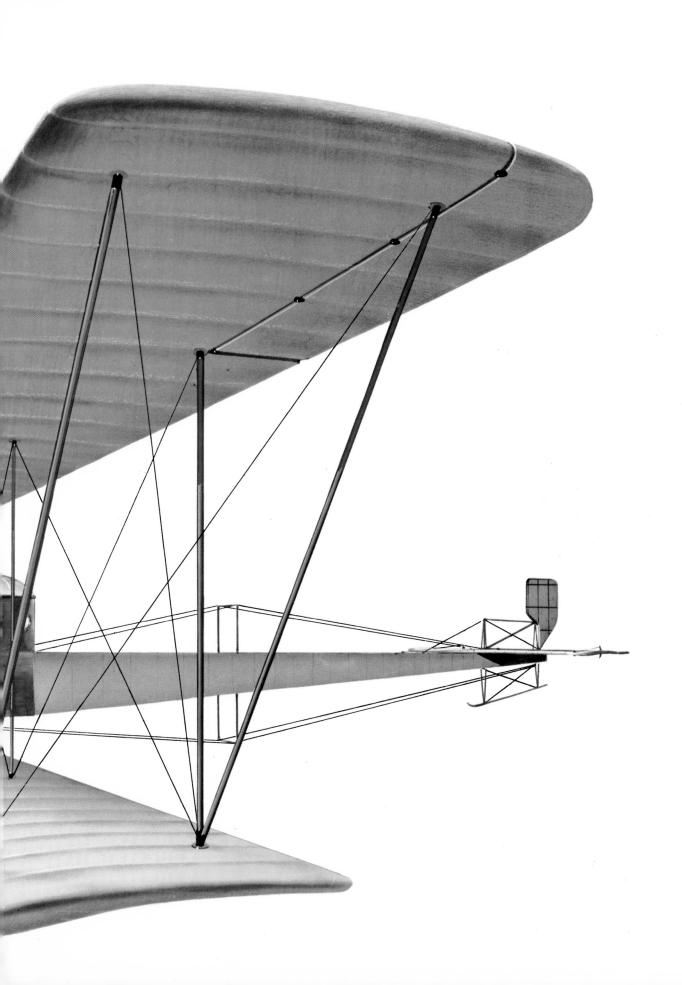

TAUBE 1912

Country: Austria. **Size:** wing span 47 ft. 1 in., 32 ft. 4 in. long,
10 ft. 4 in. high and 1,918 lbs.
Engine: one 100/120 h.p. Mercedes 6-cylinder water-cooled in-line.
Speed: 78 m.p.h.
It was a prototype design for World War I German fighters.

The inspiration for this plane came not from a bird but a palm tree. The
tree's seeds were winged and as he watched them fall, Igo Etrich felt sure
that here was an aerodynamic design he could use for a plane. His design
looked more like a bird than a flying seed. Hence its name the 'Taube',
meaning dove. In flight the graceful outline justified the name, but a
closer look revealed that the machine was covered in wires. Etrich gave up
his claim to the copyright of his design and the airplane proved to be the
father of many future planes, particularly those built for the German
First World War Air Force.

OPEL ROCKET PLANE 1929

Country: Germany. **Size:** wing span 55 ft. 8 in., 32 ft. 9 in. long.
Engine: Reaction propulsion rockets. **Speed:** 100 m.p.h.
It was the first rocket-propelled plane.

A number of leading aircraft engineers first became interested in the possibility of rocket propulsion in 1928. An aircraft was built that year and although a successful flight of about a mile was made, the plane was damaged on landing. The members of the team abandoned the joint venture, but one of them, Fritz von Opel, decided to carry on by himself, and he built this rocket-powered glider. In September 1929, with von Opel as pilot, the plane was catapulted from a cradle, and once airborne the rockets were fired.

The flight was considered successful and at one point a speed of 100 m.p.h. was reached. Curiously, tests were discontinued, but this experiment marked the world's first flight by rocket propulsion.

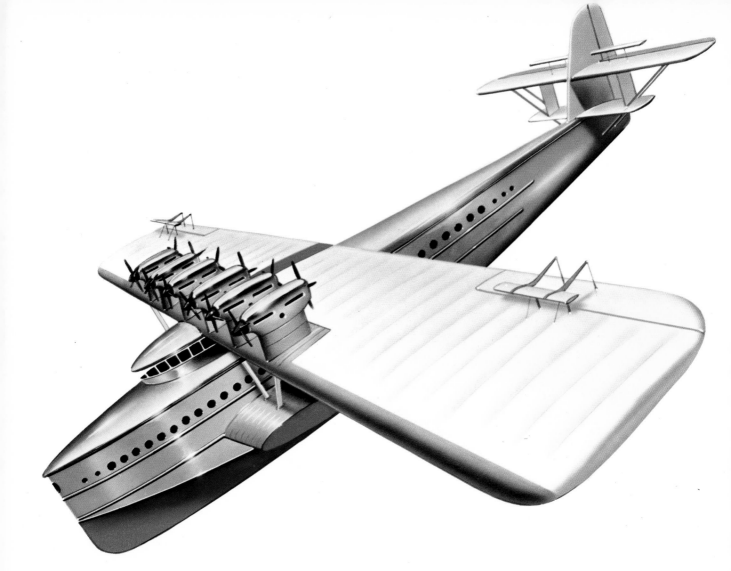

DORNIER DO X 1929

Country: Germany. **Size:** wing span 157 ft. 5 in., 13 ft. 4 in. long and 65,040 lbs. (empty), 114,640 lbs. (loaded).
Engine: Twelve 600 h.p. water-cooled Curtiss Conquerors.
Speed: 134 m.p.h.
It was one of the largest seaplanes ever built.

When it appeared in 1929, this was the world's largest aircraft ever constructed. With a load of 170 passengers and crew, its enormous bulk presented many technical problems. Radical redesign, including a complete change of engines, became necessary. Finally, on November 2, 1930, the giant seaplane began a much publicized flight from Friedrichshafen to New York. After frequent stops for repairs, the plane finally arrived in New York some ten months later, after a somewhat devious route via West Africa and South America.

Although two further aircraft were delivered to Italy, the problems encountered with its size prevented it from being a commercial success.

SUPERMARINE S6B
1931

Country: Great Britain. **Size:**
wing span 30 ft., 27 ft. 9 in. long,
12 ft. high, wing area 145 sq. ft.
and 4,560 lbs. (empty), 4,995 lbs.
(loaded).
Engine: one Rolls Royce 'R'
Sprint 2,500 h.p. **Speed:** 409
m.p.h.
**It broke the world speed
record.**

One of the best known and toughest flying events between the two world
wars was the Schneider Trophy for seaplanes. Britain first won this trophy
in 1922 and again in 1927. Then in the 1929 contest the first Supermarine
S6 appeared. The plane beat off a strong international challenge especially
from the Germans, and won the trophy again. Only one more victory in the
contest was needed to allow Britain to keep the trophy as the outright victor
and, after many modifications to the Supermarine, the S6B was entered in
the 1931 contest. There were two machines: one won the trophy, while the
other went on to raise the world speed record to 409.5 m.p.h. It was an
outstanding achievement, and the Supermarine led directly to the
development of the Second World War's most famous British fighter, the
Spitfire.

MAYO
COMPOSITE
1938

Country: Great Britain.
Flying Boat—**Size:** wing span 114 ft.,
85 ft. long, 33 ft. high and 28,000 lbs. (loaded).
Engine: Four 960 h.p. Bristol Pegasus X.

Senior Scion—**Size:** wing span 73 ft., 51 ft. long, 20 ft.
high and 20,800 lbs. (loaded).
Engine: Four 395 h.p. Napier-Halford 'Rapier'.
It was the world's first two-stage aircraft.

Dr. Mayo obtained support to build a Scion Senior
onto the back of a large Short's Empire Flying
Boat. Taking off together, they flew
to the limit of the Flying Boat's range
and the Scion was then released in
mid-air to continue the journey.
In this way the Mayo Composite
made a new record 'non-
stop' flight of 6,000
miles from Scotland
to South Africa.

GB SPORTSTER 1932

Country: U.S.A. **Size:** wing span 25 ft., 17ft. 9 in. long and 1,840 lbs. (empty), 3,075 lbs. (loaded).
Engine: one 800 h.p. wasp. **Speed:** 300 m.p.h.
It was one of the most famous air racers.

The 'golden days' of American Air Races, the 1930's, produced one of the most spectacular aircraft of all time. Designed specifically for air racing, the Gee Bees were a combination of the largest engine and the smallest bodies. The R-I (illustrated above) is undoubtedly the most famous of all, enjoying a brief but glorious history. Setting a new land plane speed record of 296.287 m.p.h., the R-I also won the much coveted Thompson Trophy race in 1932. Tragically, when competing in the 1933 transcontinental Bendix Trophy Race, the R-I suddenly went out of control and crashed upside down. R-2 met a similar fate and the remains of R-I and R-2 were pieced together to form the R-I/R-2, another formidable racer. But this crashed in 1935 at the start of another air race and thus ended a short but illustrious racing history for the Gee Bees.

POU-DE-CIEL 1935

Country: France. **Size:** wing span 19 ft. 7 in., overall length 11 ft. 6 in. and 220 lbs. (empty).
Engine: One 17 h.p. Aubier 540 cc. 2-cylinder in-line air-cooled. **Speed:** 62.1 m.p.h.
It was one of the first build-it-yourself aircraft.

Nicknamed the 'Flying Flea', the Pou-de-Ciel was yet another attempt to arouse the interest of amateurs. The ninth of a series of light aircraft designs produced by Henri Mignet, this single seat monoplane was unique in that the pilot sat underneath the wing. With the details publicized as a do-it-yourself exercise, the plane soon became popular. By the end of 1935, over 100 had been privately built in France and a series of 'Pou' clubs formed. But several fatal accidents brought this success to a rapid halt, as an inquiry showed that there was a basic defect in the aircraft's design.

AERO SPACELINES B-377, SUPER GUPPY 1965

Country: U.S.A. **Size:** wing span 141 ft. 3 in., 127 ft. long, 38 ft. 3 in. high and 145,000 lbs.
Engine: 4 Boeing turbo-prop. **Speed:** 300 m.p.h.
It transports the American moon rockets.

Possibly the world's most ugly aircraft, this plane was developed from the Boeing Strato-cruiser C97 to transport the huge stages of America's space rockets. The Super Guppy was developed entirely with private money and the U.S. Government then contracted for the exclusive use of the aircraft. The fuselage is up to 25 ft. in diameter and you can see where the nose section is hinged, so that it can swing open for easy loading. The first flight of the Super Guppy was in August 1965 and it was then proclaimed as the world's largest airplane, which in fact it still is.

CORNU HELICOPTER
1907

Country: France. **Size** 40 ft. long, rotors 20 ft. 4 in. in diameter.
Engine: One 24 h.p. Antoinette.
It was the first helicopter to fly.

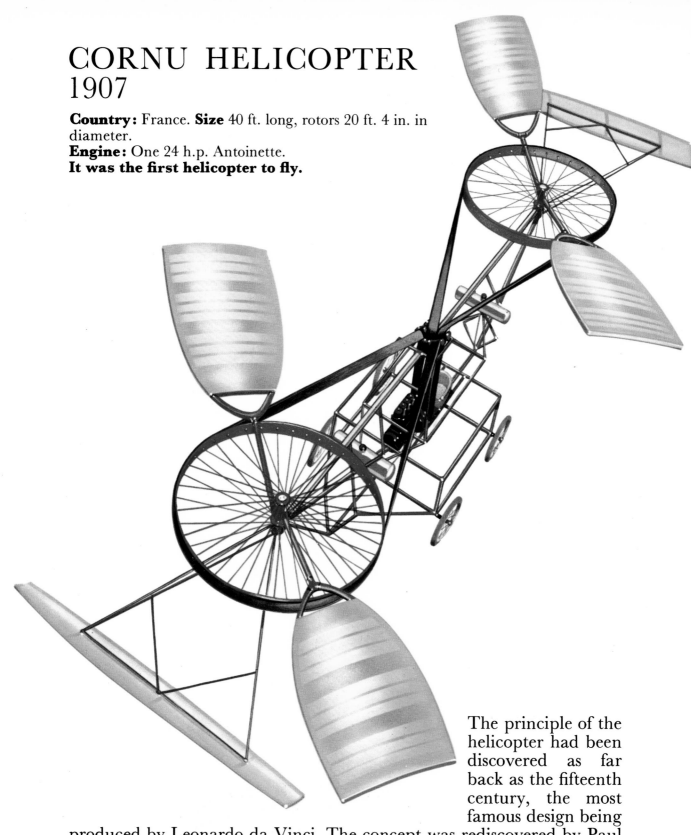

The principle of the helicopter had been discovered as far back as the fifteenth century, the most famous design being produced by Leonardo da Vinci. The concept was rediscovered by Paul Cornu and others (the Bregnet Brothers) who saw great potential in the vertical take-off, particularly with the dangers of the ever-increasing speeds necessary for conventional take-off. Paul Cornu built his machine in 1907, and tethering it to the ground to prevent it flying too high, became the first man in the world to make a free flight in a helicopter.

SIKORSKY S-64 SKYCRANE 1963

Country: U.S.A. **Size:** 88 ft. 6 in. long, 25 ft. 5 in. high and 42,000 lbs. (loaded).
Engine: 2 shaft turbines. **Speed:** 117 m.p.h.
It is one of the largest skycranes.

You have already seen Igor Sikorsky's incredible 'Le Grand' on earlier pages, but it is with helicopters that his name is most associated. Although not the world's largest helicopter, the S-64 Skycrane (known as 'Universal Lift' or 'Flying Crane') has established many records, being able to fly higher with a greater load than any other helicopter.

The military versions are equipped with interchangeable 'pods' as illustrated. Civil versions are specially designed to carry passenger coaches in an attempt to overcome the traffic problems of major cities.

ROLLS ROYCE TMR (FLYING BEDSTEAD) 1954

Country: Great Britain. **Size:** Span 14 ft., 28 ft. long, 15 ft. high and 7,196 lbs. **It was a prototype of today's vertical take-off aircraft.**

Despite the advantages of a helicopter, its forward speed is severely limited because of its large rotor blades, which serve both to propel and keep the machine airborne. The 'Flying Bedstead' was the first stage in the development of an aircraft which could take off vertically and then propel itself at supersonic speeds. A sensation was caused when this extraordinary object successfully flew in 1954, being lifted by a series of nozzles which directed the thrust of the jet engines towards the ground. This test program resulted in the development of today's highly successful Hawker Harrier Jump Jet, a tactical close support reconnaisance aircraft, which can take off from any terrain.

MIKOYAN MiG 23 (FOXBAT) 1965

Country: U.S.S.R. **Size:** wing span 40 ft., 70 ft. long.
Engine: 2 Tumansky turbo jets. **Speed:** 2,100 m.p.h.
It is one of the most advanced fighter planes.

Although not so outwardly incredible as some of the other planes in this book, the performance records of this plane are remarkable. In 1965 the Russians claimed that it had set a new World Speed Record of 1,441 m.p.h. More recent information about the plane shows that in addition to being able to fly faster than any other existing aircraft it is also able to fly higher, to a maximum ceiling of 80,000 feet. Many details still remain secret, but NATO observers have spoken of this plane as the most advanced aircraft in the world. The latest versions are now estimated to be able to fly in excess of 2,000 m.p.h. and to be armed with nuclear strike weapons.

B.A.C./SUD-AVIATION CONCORDE 1969

Country: France/Great Britain. **Size:** wing span 83 ft.
11⅛ in., 193 ft. long and 169,000 lbs. (empty).
Engine: 4 Rolls Royce Bristol/Snecma Olympus 593
turbo jets. **Speed:** 1,450 m.p.h.
It is a supersonic passenger aircraft.

Possibly the most exciting development in civil aviation, the Concorde
project is a joint development of France and Britain. A beautiful aircraft to
look at, it has a number of notable features: its wings are of a special aerodynamic design which produces optimum cruise performance; its nose
section is lowered hydraulically to improve forward view during take-off
and landing giving the famous droop-nose profile, and it has a parachute
to assist slowing down on landing. The first prototype completed by Sud-
Aviation of France flew in March 1969 and the British prototype a month
later. At present this controversial plane has only one rival, Russia's
TU144, whose design is remarkably similar. Concorde is expected to go
into service with British and French airlines in 1975 to provide the world's
first long range supersonic passenger air service, and will carry up to 128
passengers.

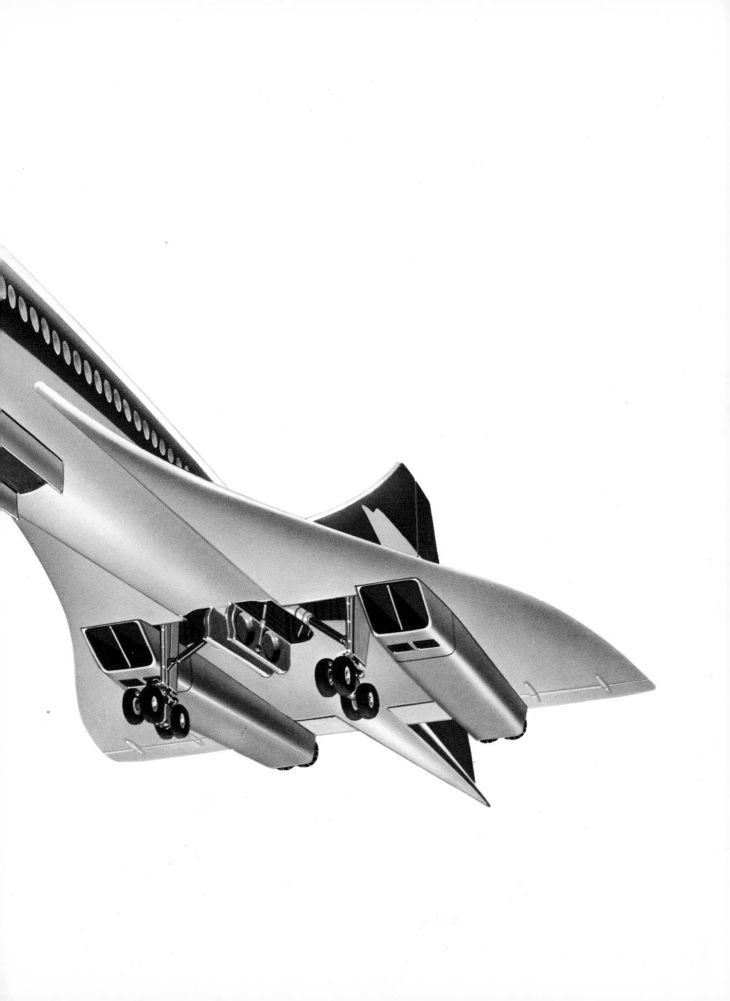

GLOSSARY

aerodynamics: studies to design wings and bodies that cause least resistance to the forces of the wind.

aerofoil: a wing-like structure, curved on the top side and flat on the bottom side.

airship: a lighter-than-air flying machine driven by an engine.

bi-plane: an aircraft with two wings, one on top of the other.

dual-control system: two sets of controls which allow either the pilot or co-pilot to control the aircraft.

fuselage: the body section of an aircraft that holds passengers and/or cargo.

jet engine: an engine that takes in air, heats it, expands it and forcibly expels it from the rear of the engine, providing forward thrust.

mono-plane: an aircraft with one wing.

rocket: a device that generates thrust by burning chemical fuels.

vacuum: a space in which there is no air and which has no pressure in it.

wind tunnel: a device used to test the effect of wind on the structure of airplanes.